GENTLE IS A GRANDMOTHER'S LOVE
© 2001 by Multnomah Publishers, Inc.
published by Multnomah Publishers, Inc.
P.O. Box 1720, Sisters, Oregon 97759

ISBN 1-58860-048-3

Artwork by Paula Vaughan is reproduced with permission from Newmark
Publishing USA.

For prints of the artwork, please contact:
Newmark Publishing USA
11700 Commonwealth Drive
Louisville, Kentucky 40299
1-800-866-5566

Designed by Koechel Peterson & Associates, Minneapolis, Minnesota

Multnomah Publishers, Inc., has made every effort to trace the ownership of all
poems and quotes. In the event of a question arising from the use of a poem or
quote, we regret any error made and will be pleased to make the necessary correction
in future editions of this book.

Please see the acknowledgments at the back of the book for complete attributions
for this material.

Scripture quotations are taken from *New American Standard Bible* (NASB) ©1960,
1977, 1995 by the Lockman Foundation. Used by permission. *The Holy Bible*, New
International Version (NIV)©1973, 1984 by International Bible Society, used by
permission of Zondervan Publishing House. *Holy Bible*, New Living Translation (NLT)
©1996. Used by permission of Tyndale House Publishers, Inc.

Multnomah is a trademark of Multnomah Publishers, Inc., and is registered in the U.S.
Patent and Trademark Office.
The colophon is a trademark of Multnomah Publishers, Inc.

Printed in China

02 03 04 05 06 — 10 9 8 7 6 5 4 3 2

www.multnomahgifts.com

Gentle Is a Grandmother's Love

Compiled by ALICE GRAY & Art by PAULA VAUGHAN

MULTNOMAH GIFTS™

Multnomah®Publishers Sisters, Oregon

Table of Contents

LEGACY OF LOVE by Alice Gray — 8

A DAY HEMMED IN LOVE by Nancy Jo Sullivan — 11

GRANDMAS MAKE A DIFFERENCE by Betty Southard — 14

LOVE IS A GRANDPARENT by Erma Bombeck — 16

LILACS TO REMEMBER by Faith Andrews Bedford — 18

BOUQUET OF LOVE by John R. Ramsey — 22

STORIES ON A HEADBOARD by Elaine Pondant — 25

A GIFT TO REMEMBER by Corrie Franz Cowart — 27

MORE BEAUTIFUL — 31

GRANDMA'S LAUGHTER by Casandra Lindell — 33

THE ATTIC DANCE by Robin Jones Gunn — 35

WHEN GRANDMA GROWS UP by Marilyn K. McAuley — 39

MOTHER EARNED HER WRINKLES by Erma Bombeck — 40

COVERED WITH PRAYER by Linda Vogel — 42

SECRET CRACKS AND CREVICES by Melody Carlson — 44

FROM THE EYES OF A CHILD — 48

THE COMFORT ROOM by Mayo Mathers — 52

GRANDMA'S GLASSES by Phil Callaway — 56

ANGEL IN UNIFORM by Jeannie Ecke Sowell — 59

STITCHES IN TIME by Philip Gulley — 61

GRANDMA'S GIFT by Wayne Rice — 64

BREAKING UP GRANDMA by Marjorie Maki — 66

WRITTEN FROM THE HEART by Bob Welch — 69

Legacy of Love

ﾟ ALICE GRAY ﾟ

As I look around our home, my heart always lingers longest on reminders that I am a grandmother.

Tiny wild violets and sunshiny dandelions, now dry and faded, brighten the corner of my desk. My granddaughter picked them one brisk morning many summers ago. With my finger I trace the barely visible crack in a silver-edged teacup, remembering our tea party. We dressed the teddy bears and ourselves in old-fashioned hats and gloves and held our pinkie fingers out daintily as we sipped sugar water tea. Inside a drawer, some of the dearest treasures are safely tucked away. I unwrap white tissue paper from a round clay plaque and measure my hand against the handprint of a four-year-old. It seems like only yesterday when I held that small hand in my own.

The years pass quickly but I am enjoying this wonderful season of being a grandmother. A newborn grandchild curls a tiny hand around grandma's finger…and a new legacy of love begins.

Once again we get to make cardboard forts in our living rooms. There's another chance to walk hand-in-small-hand on a starlit night and find the Milky Way. We can open a storybook we have saved for years and read, almost by heart, words from well-worn pages. We give sweet good-night kisses and say quiet bedtime prayers. We use names like "precious" no matter how old they get, soothe bumped knees, and offer encouragement when the way seems hard. Most of all, we help young hearts understand the great love of God.

Among all the keepsakes, I cherish one the most—not only because my granddaughter picked it out for me, but because she hugged me tight and whispered that the words were true. It is a small ceramic paperweight, shaped like an open book with gilded edges of gold, delicate pink rosebuds, and a pastel blue ribbon decorating the pages. An unknown author has written:

Grandma,
Of all the beautiful gifts
that come from heaven above,
None could be more precious
than the gift of your love.

A grandchild is a precious gift, and so is a
grandmother's love.

A Day Hemmed in Love

ᡎ Nancy Jo Sullivan ᡎ
from *Moments of Grace*

Mema was my dearly loved grandmother. She died over a decade ago, so my daughters know her mainly through what I tell them about her. I've shown them many timeworn photos. They know that Mema had a kind, wrinkled face. They also know that she tended rosebushes and collected teacups and sewed on an antique sewing machine in a cellar workshop. They know that she played an important role in my life.
"Tell us about Mema and prom day," they are fond of asking. It's their favorite Mema story.

I pulled on a string that lit a fluorescent ceiling light and stood looking around my grandmother's basement workshop. Making my way past a worktable laden with scissors and spools, I sat down at her cast-iron sewing machine. Above the machine, a wall plaque read: A Day Hemmed in Love Rarely Unravels.

It had been a month since my grandmother Mema's death. In her last moments of life, Mema had wrapped her hands around mine. Though a cancer was invading her bones, her brown eyes bore a beautiful sheen, polished from years of smiling.

"Come back for the sewing machine…it's yours," she had said.

Now, as I opened the bottom drawer of the sewing machine cabinet, I found a collection of fabric swatches, saved patches from treasures that Mema had once sewn for my family.

Although there were piles of gingham and wool and lace squares, a piece of green floral voile caught my eye. As I took the patch into my hand, I forgot that I was a wife and mother of three; now I was seventeen years old, and it was the morning of my senior prom.

Clomping down the stairs that led to Mema's sewing room, my face streaming with exaggerated teenage tears, I plopped my gown on her worktable.

"It looks awful," I wailed.

Mema put on her bifocals, carefully examining the formal I had sewn. The hem was crooked. The waistline was puckering. Threads hung from uneven seams.

Mema shook her head when she saw that I had lined the sheer green flowered bodice with bright yellow satin.

"There wasn't any green lining left; I didn't think the yellow would show through," I whimpered. "All it needs is the loving touch," Mema said as she held a tape measure to a mismatched sleeve.

For the rest of the day, Mema and I worked side by side at her sewing machine, her shoe tapping the foot pedal as a spool of thread whirled and a needle stitched in a buzz of rhythm.

As Mema mended raveling seams, she reminisced about her past, the hard times of the Depression, losing the farm, the war.

"I sewed your mom's clothes," Mema remembered.

As I handed her pins, I nodded, but I had heard all the stories before.

Preoccupied with the present, I began to chatter on and on about my date for the prom.

"I think he likes me more than I like him," I admitted.

"Maybe the dress will scare him off," Mema joked. We laughed.

When at last the final seams of the formal were sewn, Mema held the dress up to my shoulders.

"Try it on." She looked hopeful, her brown eyes twinkling.

As I donned the refashioned gown, I danced my way past her sewing machine, my hand grazing the back of my hair like a runway fashion model. Though the yellow lining still didn't quite go with the sheer green florals, Mema's impeccable sewing had transformed my dress into a fashion statement.

"You look beautiful." Mema grinned, her aging face a sweet, unforgettable mixture of crow's-feet and smile wrinkles.

"Love you," I said as I kissed her good-bye and rushed home to get ready for the dance.

That night, my date came to the door with a huge bright pink corsage. He didn't mind that the flowers didn't match my yellow and green gown, he just kept saying how beautiful I looked.

I laughed to myself as I remembered Mema's words, "maybe the dress will scare him off." As we drove to the prom in an expensive limousine, I got up the nerve to tell him I just wanted to be friends. "That's okay, let's just have fun," he said.

At the dance we mingled with other teenage friends dressed in tuxedos and gowns. We laughed and danced and ate fancy hors d'oeuvres. Everyone told me how funky my dress looked.

Though it was a memorable night, I can't seem to remember what color tux my date wore or where we went to dinner or even where the prom was held. What I do remember about prom day was the special time I spent with Mema. She had given me a memory to tuck away in my heart for a lifetime, like a precious patch of fabric saved for years in a drawer. I would never forget the laughter we shared, the stories I heard, or the age-old wisdom that had rescued me from certain dress disaster. Her presence in my young life was a thread of love that would never be broken.

I slipped the prom dress patch into my pocket and lifted the sewing machine from the cabinet, carefully placing it into a case I could carry.

I took one last look around Mema's workshop. I wanted to remember the way it looked: the scissors, the spools, and the plaque on the wall.

I wanted to remember A Day Hemmed in Love Rarely Unravels.

～❧～

Have courage for the great sorrows of life and patience for the small ones; and when you have laboriously accomplished your daily task, go to sleep in peace. God is awake.

Victor Hugo

Grandmas Make a Difference

⌘ BETTY SOUTHARD ⌘

The photo studio was packed with mommies in line and kids everywhere. As my daughter waited her turn to see the proofs of the photos taken the week before, I was playing and laughing with Elizabeth, my eighteen-month-old granddaughter. I soon noticed a little black-haired girl standing alone across the room. Her huge dark eyes never left Elizabeth and me. No one was paying attention to her and my grandmother's heart reached out.

"Hi!" I said. "What's your name?"

The child dropped her head, shuffled her feet, and mumbled something softly.

"What?" I asked. "I didn't hear you."

The reaction was the same. I wondered if perhaps she didn't speak English and didn't understand me. I smiled and started to turn my attention back to Elizabeth when the little girl's demeanor suddenly changed.

Holding her head high, standing tall, and looking me directly in the eye, she spoke loud and clear: "But Grandma calls me Precious!"

A Four-Year-Old's Prayers

A mother was listening to her four-year-old's prayers.
The little girl softly went through all the "God bless yous."
Then in a very loud voice asked for a brand-new red bike
for her birthday.
"God isn't deaf, dear," the mother said.
"I know! But Grandma's way out in the living room and she's
the one who's giving me the bike."

AUTHOR UNKNOWN

Love Is a Grandparent

⮞ Erma Bombeck ⮜

A preschooler who lives down the street was curious about grandparents. It occurred to me that, to a child, grandparents appear like an apparition with no explanation, no job description and few credentials. They just seem to go with the territory.

This, then, is for the little folks who wonder what a grandparent is.

A grandparent can always be counted on to buy all your cookies, flower seeds, all-purpose greeting cards, transparent tape, paring knives, peanut brittle and ten chances on a pony. (Also a box of taffy when they have dentures.)

A grandparent helps you with the dishes when it is your night.

A grandparent is the only baby-sitter who doesn't charge more after midnight—or anything before midnight.

A grandparent buys you gifts your mother says you don't need.

A grandparent arrives three hours early for your baptism, your graduation and your wedding because she wants a seat where she can see everything.

A grandparent loves you from when you're a bald baby to a bald father and all the hair in between.

A grandparent will put a sweater on you when she is cold, feed you when she is hungry and put you to bed when she is tired.

A grandparent will brag on you when you get a typing pin that eighty other girls got.

A grandparent will frame a picture of your hand that you traced and put it in her Mediterranean living room.

A grandparent will slip you money just before Mother's Day.

A grandparent will help you with your buttons, your zippers and your shoelaces and not be in any hurry for you to grow up.

When you're a baby, a grandparent will check to see if you are crying when you are sound asleep.

When a grandchild says, "Grandma, how come you didn't have any children?" a grandparent holds back the tears.

Grandchildren are the crowning
glory of the aged.

PROVERBS 17:6, NLT

Lilacs to Remember

FAITH ANDREWS BEDFORD

The soft spring air is full of the fragrance of the year's first mowing. Neat golden bales dot the meadow, and the fruit trees look as though they've been frosted with vanilla icing. As I stand on my porch and look out across the valley to the mountaintops beyond, I can see that the light green of new leaves has pushed up the slopes and almost reached the peaks. It is time for the first wildflower walk of the season.

My husband and I take our pickup along an old logging trail that winds its way up the mountainside. As we bounce over rocks and displace loose gravel, pale pink mountain laurel branches brush against the windows. The road ends beneath a tangle of wild rhododendron. We lace up our hiking boots and fill our water jugs from a spring that burbles up from beneath a mossy rock.

As we walk, we spot trillium and lady's slippers, false Solomon's seal and dogtooth violets. Sun-warmed pine needles release their pungent fragrance as we maneuver beneath the drooping boughs of the tall trees.

A faint path leads off into a hemlock wood. We have passed it before but never taken it; this time, we decide to explore. Presently, the forest begins to open up and ahead we can see the light of a clearing. In the center rises a stone chimney, a remnant of an abandoned homestead.

I smell the lilacs before I see them. The breeze is suddenly rich and sweet. Beside the chimney we find an old root cellar ringed with periwinkle; blue blossoms pale against shiny green leaves. Next to a broad flat rock, which must have served as a front step, stands a lilac bush, its thick, gnarled branches laden with deep purple spires. I draw some to me. The scent envelops me and, for a moment, I am no longer in a forest clearing but in my grandmother's garden.

Lilacs were her favorite flower; her yard was ringed with them. But it was not until I was nine or ten that I discovered that one of the shrubs was mine. On a soft spring afternoon much like this one, Grandmother and I were gathering flowers for her dining room. As I reached up to clip the white lilac she said, "That's your lilac, you know." I turned around in surprise.

She smiled. "Yes, I planted that in your honor the year you were born." I regarded the lovely shrub, which was far taller than I was, and felt very important.

Then Grandmother took my hand and introduced me to all of the other lilacs in her garden. As we stood beneath the largest one she said, "I planted this one the year Jimmy was born." ("Jimmy" was my father. It always startled me to hear anyone call that tall, balding man Jimmy. Mother called him Jim.)

We moved on to a wine red lilac. "And this one I planted in memory of your grandfather the year he died." Her smile faded for a moment, then she led me toward the front yard. By the gate was a deep pink lilac just a bit taller than mine.

"This one I planted the year your parents were married," Grandmother said. "It certainly has thrived." Indeed it had. Several boughs were so heavy with blooms that Grandmother had to prop them up with forked branches pruned from her apple tree.

Behind the flower bed were two small lilacs, one light lavender and one pale pink. "These I planted for your sisters," she said, clipping a sprig from each and placing them in her basket. "The lavender one is Ellen's; it is called 'Minuet.' The little pink one is called 'Moonglow'; I planted it three years ago for Beth."

My little sisters were only six and three, but I couldn't wait to tell them that they had their very own lilacs in Grandmother's garden—lilacs with beautiful names.

As we drew close to the terrace, I saw a small lilac bush with just a few tiny blooms. They were the blue of an evening sky and their scent was exotic, almost spicy. I had not seen the bush before. I looked up at Grandmother.

"That one is called 'Nocturne,'" she said, "and I planted it for myself last fall in honor of my retirement from the library." She laughed and added, "I thought I deserved it."

For years, Grandmother had helped the children of our village find the perfect book. Now she would be able to spend her days doing what she loved best: reading and gardening.

For many years, our lilacs, as I came to regard them, filled both her house and ours with fragrant arrangements. At my wedding, I carried a bouquet that Grandmother had fashioned from my lilac bush.

By the time my first child was born, Grandmother could no longer garden. When I told her of Drew's birth she said, "Plant a lilac for him, won't you, dear?" And I promised that I would.

But it was many years before we had a home of our own. Though I planted lilacs for my children, we kept moving and leaving their lilacs behind. By the time we settled down, my firstborn was in high school. I had forgotten about the lilacs.

Now, surrounded once again by the sweet scent of a lilac in bloom, I remember Grandmother and my promise to her. Drew became a father last month; his new daughter, Carter Elisabeth, has his pale hair and blue eyes. I resolve to plant a lilac in honor of her birth and in memory of her great-great grandmother.

As we turn to walk back, I break off a small branch from the lilac bush and tuck it into my hatband. The earthy dampness beneath my feet mingled with the scent of lilac is like a garden after rain.

When I get back home, I shall take down my gardening books and find just the right lilac for my new granddaughter and my grandmother. Perhaps "Vestale," a white one like the one Grandmother planted for me, or maybe "Primrose," an outstanding pale yellow lilac just the color of Carter's hair. It must be perfect, this lilac for a first grandchild. It will grow and flourish and then, some spring when she comes to visit, I will pluck for her a bouquet of sweet-scented blossoms from her very own lilac bush. And she will feel very important.

❧❦❧

She offers you life in her right hand,
and riches and honor in her left.
She will guide you down delightful
paths; all her ways are satisfying.

PROVERBS 3:16–17, NLT

21

Bouquet of Love

John R. Ramsey

For some time a person has provided me with a rose boutonniere to pin on the lapel of my suit every Sunday. Because I always got a flower on Sunday morning, I really did not think much of it. It was a nice gesture that I appreciated, but it became routine. One Sunday, however, what I considered ordinary became very special.

As I was leaving the Sunday service a young man approached me. He walked right up to me and said, "Sir, what are you going to do with your flower?" At first I did not know what he was talking about but then I understood.

I said, "Do you mean this?" as I pointed to the rose pinned to my coat.

He said, "Yes, sir. I would like it if you are just going to throw it away." At this point I smiled and gladly told him that he could have my flower, casually asking him what he was going to do with it. The little boy, who was probably less than ten years old, looked up at me and said, "Sir, I'm going to give it to my granny. My mother and father got divorced last year. I was living with my mother, but when she married again, she wanted me to live with my father. I lived with him for a while, but he said I could not stay, so he sent me to live with my grandmother. She is so good to me. She cooks for me and takes care of me. She has been so good to me that I want to give that pretty flower to her for loving me."

When the little boy finished I could hardly speak. My eyes filled with tears and I knew I had been touched in the depths of my soul. I reached up and unpinned my flower. With the flower in my hand, I looked at the boy and said, "Son, that is the nicest thing I have ever heard, but you can't have just this flower because it's not enough. If you'll look in front of the pulpit, you'll see a big bouquet of flowers. Please take those flowers to your granny because she deserves the very best."

If I hadn't been touched enough already, he made one last statement and I will always cherish it. He said, "What a wonderful day! I asked for one flower but got a beautiful bouquet."

Life is short, and we never have too much time for gladdening the hearts of those who are traveling the dark journey with us.
O be swift to love, make haste to be kind!

Amiel

Stories on a Headboard

Elaine Pondant

Reprinted wth permission from the
March 1994 *Reader's Digest*

The bed was about forty-five years old when Mom passed it along to me a few months after my father died. I decided to strip the wood and finish it for my daughter Melanie. The headboard was full of scratches.

Just before starting to take the paint off, I noticed that one of the scratches was a date: September 18, 1946, the day my parents were married. Then it struck me—this was the first bed they had as husband and wife!

Right above their wedding date was another name and date: "Elizabeth, October 22, 1947."

My mother answered the phone. "Who is Elizabeth," I asked, "and what does October 22, 1947, mean?"

"She's your sister."

I knew Mom had lost a baby, but I never saw this as anything more than a misfortune for my parents. After all, they went on to have five more children.

"You gave her a name?" I asked.

"Yes. Elizabeth has been watching us from heaven for forty-five years. She's as much a part of me as any of you."

"Mom, there are a lot of dates and names I don't recognize on the headboard."

"June 8, 1959?" Mom asked.

"Yes. It says 'Sam.'"

"Sam was a black man who worked for your father at the plant. Your father was fair with everyone, treating those under him with equal respect, no matter what their race or religion. But there was a lot of racial tension at that time. There was also a union strike and a lot of trouble.

"One night some strikers surrounded your dad before he got to his car. Sam showed up with several friends, and the crowd dispersed. No one was hurt. The strike eventually ended, but your dad never forgot Sam. He said Sam was an answer to his prayer."

"Mom, there are other dates on the headboard. May I come over and talk to you about them?" I sensed the headboard was full of stories. I couldn't just strip and sand them away.

Over lunch, Mom told me about January 14, 1951, the day she lost her purse at a department store. Three days later, the purse arrived in the mail. A letter from a woman named Amy said: "I took five dollars from your wallet to mail the purse to you. I hope you will understand." There was no return address, so Mom couldn't thank her, and there was nothing missing except the five dollars.

Then there was George. On December 15, 1967, George shot a rattlesnake poised to strike my brother Dominick. On September 18, 1971, my parents celebrated their silver wedding anniversary and renewed their vows.

I learned about a nurse named Janet who stayed by my mother and prayed with her after my sister Patricia's near-fatal fall from a swing. There was a stranger who broke up the attempted mugging of my father but left without giving his name.

"Who is Ralph?" I asked.

"On February 18, 1966, Ralph saved your brother's life in Da Nang. Ralph was killed two years later on his second tour of duty."

My brother never spoke about the Vietnam War. The memories were deeply buried. My nephew's name is Ralph. Now I knew why.

"I almost stripped away these remarkable stories," I said. "How could you give this headboard to me?"

"Your dad and I carved our first date on the headboard the night we married. From then on, it was a diary of our life together. When Dad died, our life together was over. But the memories never die."

When I told my husband about the headboard, he said, "There's room for a lot more stories."

We moved the bed with the storybook headboard into our room. My husband and I have already carved in three dates and names: Barbara and Greg and Jackson. Someday, we'll tell Melanie the stories from her grandparents' lives. And someday the bed will pass on to her.

A Gift to Remember

∽ CORRIE FRANZ COWART ∽

Sometimes we find threads of life that bind generation to generation. Sometimes there are symbols that make family history alive in the present. When I sit down to play my grandfather's piano I feel this thrill. I hear him playing evening lullabies to my mother, passionate Beethoven for my grandmother, and playful jigs for me to dance to. Grandfather Lester's piano is a symbol of abiding love.

The son of a small-town preacher, Lester was not born into great worldly wealth. Rather than money, he received a virtuous upbringing in which he learned the values of self-reliance and undying resolve, and found his joy in the creative aspects of life. Captivated by his love of music, Lester chopped cords of wood to earn piano lessons.

The Depression meant an end to my grandpa's college education, as well as his musical pursuits. He was thirty when he married his sweetheart, Frances, and the two of them began to make the sweet domestic harmony of a little home and family. Lester's interest in music never subsided. Whenever he could, he listened to and studied the great classical composers. He didn't, however, have much of an opportunity to practice his own talents. With many bills to be paid and the prospect of children on the way, purchasing a piano for himself just was not practical or realistic.

In 1942 he was drafted and sent to the European front lines. Every day, amid the horrors of war, Lester found time to write to his dearest Frances. He longed to be home with her and the "little man," the name he gave their newborn son, in the "little mansion," the title he bestowed on their modest home. His cherished correspondence, carefully preserved, was read and reread, as every day Frances would anxiously await his next letter.

Lester sent all the money he could to support his young family, while Frances worked part time as a nurse to help make ends meet. Scrimping and saving, she lived on the bare necessities, praying continually for her husband's safety.

Then one day in March 1946, with the war over and Europe finally secured, Lester returned to his family in the "little mansion." To his surprise a gift of love awaited him. All the checks he had sent to feed his small family had been carefully saved to buy a gift to feed his soul. My grandmother, forgoing comfort for herself, had saved nearly every penny to buy a piano for her beloved husband. It was just a small spinet, but to Lester it could not look or sound better than the world's finest concert grand.

Though Grandpa Lester and Grandma Frances have passed from this earth, every note from this instrument sings of my grandparents' love for one another and their love for me still. It is music that connects across seas, through generations and beyond death.

You will find, as you look back
upon your life,
that the moments when you
have really lived
are the moments when you
have done things
in the spirit of love.

HENRY DRUMMOND

Life is no brief candle to me. It is a sort of splendid torch which I have got hold of for the moment, and I want to make it burn as brightly as possible before handing it on to future generations.

GEORGE BERNARD SHAW

More Beautiful
～ Author Unknown ～

The question is asked, "Is there anything more beautiful in life than a boy and girl clasping clean hands and pure hearts in the path of marriage? Can there be anything more beautiful than young love?"

And the answer is given. "Yes, there is a more beautiful thing. It is the spectacle of an old man and an old woman finishing their journey together on the path. Their hands are gnarled, but still clasped; their faces are seamed, but still radiant; their hearts are physically bowed and tired, but still strong with love and devotion for one another. Yes, there is a more beautiful thing than young love. Old love."

Grandma's Laughter

❧ Casandra Lindell ❧

Violets and roses will always be soft, happy flowers to me because they were my grandmother's favorite—and my grandmother always laughed.

Small pots of violets covered a two-level table in the living room. They must have known she loved them because they were always in bloom. I can see her in my mind's eye, carefully picking off spotted leaves and smiling the flowers from their stems. She did the same thing with people—smiling, encouraging, carefully tending. Roses bordered the entire yard and Grandma tended them carefully with the same smile. Throughout the spring and summer Grandpa regularly cut armfuls of roses for the house. He kept the tables full of bouquets in cut glass vases. Any visitor could count on taking home a handful of roses from the yard.

But visitors took home more than roses—they took home Grandma's laughter. She "got tickled" when she was lost and drove in circles looking for an address. She smiled with warmth to match the main course as she put the last of the evening meal on the table. She laughed in delight as she cuddled me while I told her a story. She giggled when hummingbirds fluttered outside the dining room window.

When Grandma dropped a glass bottle of maple syrup in the grocery store, she smiled and said she felt clumsy. She turned to call someone to clean it up and stepped in the syrup. She slipped, fell, and broke her wrist. As she lay there on her back, propped on her unbroken arm to keep from lying on a shard of glass, Grandma started laughing. She laughed while the employees helped her up. She laughed as she waited for the ambulance, and she laughed when she told the story even years later.

When she died, my five-year-old nephew wanted to say good-bye, and he didn't quite understand what that meant. My sister told him, the best she could, that he wouldn't be able to sit in Grandma's lap and she wouldn't tell him stories anymore. Tommy drew a picture and his dad helped him write "I'll miss you, Grandma. It's okay to cry," across the top.

"Mommy?" His big eyes were questioning, his brow puzzled. "I won't hear her laughing, will I?" Like Tommy, I thought I would miss Grandma's laughter most of all.

Until four months later. I sat at Grandma's dining room table, painting a vase as I waited for Grandpa to come home. As I reached to pick up the phone, my sleeve caught the container of black paint and swept it off the table—to land upside down on the carpet.

"That's okay," I heard myself say out loud in a sweet and gentle tone not quite my own. "Clean it up as best you can. It's an old carpet." And then I started laughing. I laughed at my clumsiness and at the black smear that just seemed to spread despite my best efforts. I giggled at the mass of paper towels piling up in the garbage bag. And then I sat back and laughed in delight at a full grown little girl who had learned to find delight in even the messiest situations.

I almost looked up to see if Grandma was standing there—and then I realized that Grandma's laughter was still with me.

‿◦◦◦

"She made home happy!"

HENRY COLE

The Attic Dance

ᴗ Robin Jones Gunn ᴗ

Dear Sis,

    Well, you're right again! We arrived at Uncle Chuck and Aunt Pat's yesterday afternoon, and very little has changed here since we were kids. Pat is as sweet and soft and full of smiles as ever. Rachel took to her immediately, and began calling her "Gramma Pat."

    Our tour of the garden produced a whole basketful of fresh string beans. Gramma Pat showed Rachel how to snap the ends of the beans while I clipped the last of the gardenias from the bush next to the clothesline. The bush is *huge* now—at least a foot over my head. And the gardenias are as fragrant as the ones I carried in my wedding. Remember that bouquet? Yesterday I had another one just like it.

    Rachel was thrilled to find that Gramma Pat has "a real attic." You wouldn't believe the stuff she has up there! Think of Mom's sewing room when we lived on 14th Street—only with trunks instead of tidy, stacked bins. Pat let Rachel open one of the large, barrel-top trunks and look inside. Rachel's face lit up the room! You'd have thought she had discovered buried treasure. The trunk brimmed with an assortment of faded, crumpled, fancy dresses. I stood there in the heat and dust, barely able to breathe.

    But Rachel was in heaven.

    "Where'd you get this one, Gramma Pat?" Rachel asked.

    "The blue one? Oh my. I wore that to the Indian Summer Dance at the lake when I was seventeen."

    Rachel pulled out a yellowed gown with a moth-eaten collar made of rabbit fur. Pat said it was from the Christmas Ball when she was crowned the second runner-up for Snow Princess.

"What about this one?" Rachel extracted a short, black taffeta dance skirt. It had layers of netting that made it stick out. The waistband was torn on the side. It was from some sort of "Nights in Paris" dance revue. Pat said she lost the magenta bolero that went with it. I felt like muttering, "Oh, too bad."

But Rachel was in awe. "It's the most beautiful skirt in the whole world!" she said. Pat told her to try it on, and we were immediately treated to a lively performance of twirls and curtsies. The skirt hadn't had a workout like that in fifty years. As we watched Rachel dance, utterly charmed in spite of the new clouds of dust, I told Pat, "I can see now why you kept all this stuff."

She laughed at me and said, "Oh, that's not why I kept them. I kept them so I'd know it wasn't all a dream."

I wish you could have seen her face when she said those words. The years seemed to roll away for a moment when she smiled. Her eyes got all sparkly and dewy. I watched her tuck the snow princess dress back in the trunk, and I felt quite sure that she still has a dream or two spinning in that lovely head of hers.

We leave in the morning. Our plan is to make it to Atlanta by late afternoon. We'll see how far we get. Do you know what keeps going through my mind? That I'll wake up sometime next February and this whole summer trip with Rachel will seem just like a dream.

But then…all I'll really have to do is check Rachel's closet for the frilly taffeta skirt, and I'll know we were really there. Yes, "Gramma Pat" told Rachel she could take the "most beautiful skirt in the whole world" home with her. Rachel plans to wear it in the car all the way to Atlanta.

I know what you're saying! Too bad the matching magenta bolero is missing.

With love and a hug,
Robin

When Grandma Grows Up

❧ MARILYN K. McAULEY ❧

Danny was only three when he and his daddy came to live with us for a year. Every morning we would stand at the door and throw kisses and wave good-bye as Grandpa and Daddy left for their jobs. Then Danny and Grandma would get the house in order so we could build skyscrapers with building blocks and journey into wonderful places reading book after book. Later we would walk our country lane out to the highway to get the mail each day and listen to the wind whisper through the tall fir trees.

After work one evening, Grandpa swung Danny in the air and said, "Let's go get a hamburger." As we drove three-quarters of an hour to town we sang and talked and then it grew quiet. Danny was thinking. He said, "Grandpa has a job and Daddy has a job and when I grow up, I'll have a job."

"That's right, Danny," said Grandpa.

After a little more thought, Danny added, "And when Grandma grows up she'll get a job too."

❧❧❧

If we had known grandkids were so much fun,
we'd have had them first.

AUTHOR UNKNOWN

Mother Earned Her Wrinkles

∽ ERMA BOMBECK ∽
from *Forever, Erma*

According to her height and weight on the insurance charts, she should be a guard for the Lakers.

She has iron-starved blood, one shoulder is lower than the other, and she bites her fingernails.

She is the most beautiful woman I have ever seen. She should be. She's worked on that body and face for more than sixty years. The process for that kind of beauty can't be rushed.

The wrinkles on her face have been earned …one at a time. The stubborn one around the lips that deepened with every "No!" The thin ones on the forehead that mysteriously appeared when the first child was born.

The eyes are protected by glass now, but you can still see the perma-crinkles around them. Young eyes are darting and fleeting. These are mature eyes that reflect a lifetime. Eyes that have glistened with pride, filled with tears of sorrow, snapped in anger and burned from loss of sleep. They are now direct and penetrating and look at you when you speak.

The bulges are classics. They developed slowly from babies too sleepy to walk who had to be carried home from Grandma's, grocery bags lugged from the car, ashes carried out of the basement while her husband was at war. Now they are fed by a minimum of activity, a full refrigerator and TV bends.

The extra chin is custom-grown and takes years to perfect. Sometimes you can only see it from the side, but it's there. Pampered women don't have an extra chin. They cream them away or pat the muscles until they become firm. But this chin has always been there, supporting a nodding head that has slept in a chair all night…bent over knitting…praying.

The legs are still shapely, but the step is slower. They ran too often for the bus, stood a little too long when she clerked in a department store, got beat up while teaching her daughter how to ride a two-wheeler. They're purple at the back of the knees.

The hands? They're small and veined and have been dunked, dipped, shook, patted, wrung, caught in doors, splintered, dyed, bitten and blistered, but you can't help but be impressed when you see the ring finger that has shrunk from years of wearing the same wedding ring. It takes time—and much more—to diminish a finger.

I looked at Mother long and hard the other day and said, "Mom, I have never seen you look so beautiful."

"I work at it," she snapped.

As a white candle in a holy place,
So is the beauty of an aged face.

JOSEPH CAMPBELL

Covered with Prayer

Linda Vogel

My precious one,

In celebration of your arrival I've made you a special gift, called a prayer blanket. When you are covered with it, know that you are covered in prayer. Each tiny stitch represents a prayer prayed for you. Here are my ten prayers for you:

1. Like a ball of yarn that turns into a beautiful blanket, God has a beautiful plan for your life.

I pray you discover it (Jeremiah 1:5).

2. This blanket is made with my human hands. But you are "fearfully and wonderfully made" by divine hands.

I pray you will know how special you are to God (Psalm 139:14).

3. If I miss a stitch, the blanket will unravel. God has wonderful plans for every step of your life.

I pray you will look to Him for His plan and know that even when we as your family miss a stitch or make a mistake, God can redeem that as we trust Him (Proverbs 28:13).

4. If I go back and correct a stitch, the blanket won't be "holey." If you go back and confess your sins, your life will be holy.

I pray you will have the courage to confess wrongdoing so you can live a holy life (1 John 1:9).

5. This blanket has many stitches, but they are nothing compared to the number of thoughts God has toward you.

I pray you will think about God and know He thinks about you (Psalm 139:17).

6. It took three strands wrapped together to make a strong yarn for this blanket. It will take three parts (you, your family, and God) to make a strong life for you. And it will take three divine parts of God to keep you together.

I pray you will depend on God and your family (Ecclesiastes 4:12).

7. The border on this blanket protects the blanket from becoming misshapen. God wants to put a border around your life to keep you safe from harm.

I pray you will stay within the borders God sets for you (Job 1:10).

8. My hope for this prayer blanket is to keep you warm and secure. How much more is God's plan! He wants to give you a "future and hope."

I pray you will always put your hope in God (Jeremiah 29:11).

9. When you are covered by this blanket, know you are covered in love and prayer. God wants to also cover you with the love of His Son.

I pray you will come to love Jesus at an early age (John 14:21).

10. Although you will outgrow this blanket, *I pray you will never want to outgrow your need for God (1 John 4:1–17).*

Love,
Your grandmother

Secret Cracks and Crevices

~ Melody Carlson ~

Grandma's tall Victorian house looked like a castle to me as a child. Proud and white, it roosted on a grassy knoll skirted by a colorful flower bed. Total strangers would pause to admire and even photograph Grandma's striking rock garden. But the three-hour trip to Grandma's house amounted to more than merely visiting her turreted home with its gingerbread trim and pretty flowers; it meant entering a world unlike my everyday one.

At Grandma's, everything changed, and I encountered a secret world—a world where only I knew all the fascinating nooks and crannies. I could dawdle away countless summer hours exploring its hidden corners. I remember the warm, earthy smell after a summer shower and the feel of the cool, damp concrete through my thin cotton shorts as I sat on the steps behind Grandma's house.

Lush, leafy fuchsia plants profuse with luxuriant purplish flowers overflowed the deep beds that bordered those steps. They looked like miniature Japanese lanterns, and the honeybees scurried about them gathering food. I remember the waxen feel of an unopened fuchsia blossom and the pop it made when pinched gently by my fingers—and the muffled, angry buzz of the unfortunate bee I imprisoned in the royal-colored depths of a bloom.

I would climb up those fuchsia-bordered steps to the home of Martha—Grandma's neighbor. Her flagstone patio, still wet from the rain, steamed and glistened in the afternoon sun. Beside her patio grew a small garden surrounded by a child-sized fence. I'd stand and lean my arms upon it and inspect the mysterious green foliage flourishing within. A clothesline stretched high over the garden. On one end hung a pulley my grandpa had designed to draw the flapping whites to and fro without having to set foot in Martha's garden. Martha and Grandma shared the line, dividing the sunshine between them.

Inside her sun-filled front room, Martha kept building blocks and wooden dolls, picture books and an old 3-D photo viewer—all for her young visitors. Of course, cookies and tea would invariably be served; it was a little girl's utopia.

Down the street lived Grandma's sister, Londy. Londy's house reminded me of Snow White's cottage. Surrounded by towering trees and tucked in so neatly, it might have sprouted like an oversized mushroom. Londy, a tiny woman, fit flawlessly with her diminutive house. She liked to bustle about and prepare delectable snacks in her compact kitchen. She'd array toast and homemade preserves on flowery china for her much-welcomed guests, and she never discriminated between children and adults—we all ate from the same dainty dishes; no plastic was found in her kitchen.

Londy enjoyed cut flowers, and they often cascaded from the porcelain vases in her home. Outside her kitchen window grew roses, berry bushes, and mint. The mixture of their fragrances was almost intoxicating as it wafted in on a warm summer breeze. Londy's home felt like an enchanted, full-grown dollhouse.

At Grandma's house, I'd be the first one up in the morning because I knew Grandpa had breakfast sizzling and steaming downstairs in the cozy kitchen.

After eating, I'd linger at the table in front of the big picture window, where the bright red geraniums bloomed year round in the window box. I'd try to spy the little green frog who lived in the geraniums and watch the hummingbirds flitter about the hanging flower baskets. Summers were timeless then—no schedule, no routine.

Although the places remain, the people are gone, and I'm torn between the desire to return and discover what time has done to my childhood paradise and the fear that the spell, now broken, would only bring disappointment. For the places I remember, even if they have remained unchanged, can never be found again because my child's eye perceived the hill as a mountain and the house as a castle.

And so these memories must continue to endure in the secret places—hidden in the cracks and crevices—only to be visited through remembering.

Where we love is home,
home that our feet may leave,
but not our hearts.

OLIVER WENDELL HOLMES

From the Eyes of a Child
✑ Author Unknown ✑

A grandmother is a lady who has no children of her own. She likes other people's little girls and boys. A grandfather is a man grandmother. He goes for walks with the boys, and they talk about fishing and stuff like that.

Grandmothers don't have to do anything except to be there. They're so old that they shouldn't play hard or run. It is enough if they drive us to the market where the pretend horse is, and have lots of dimes ready. Or if they take us for walks, they should slow down past things like pretty leaves and caterpillars. They should never say "hurry up."

Usually, grandmothers are fat, but not too fat to tie your shoes. They wear glasses and funny underwear. They can take their teeth and gums off.

Grandmothers don't have to be smart, only answer questions like, "Why isn't God married?" and "How come dogs chase cats?"

Grandmothers don't talk baby talk like visitors do, because it is hard to understand. When they read to us they don't skip or mind if it is the same story over again.

Everybody should try to have a grandmother, especially if they don't have a television, because they are the only grown-ups who have time.

Grandmother's Wisdom

I long to put the experience of fifty years at once into your young lives, to give you at once the key of that treasure chamber every gem of which has cost me tears and struggles and prayer, but you must work for these inward treasures yourself.

HARRIET BEECHER STOW

∼∽∽∼

Hope is the companion of power, and mother of success; for who so hopes strongly has within him the gift of miracles.

SAMUEL SMILES

Just being happy is a fine thing to do;
Looking on the bright side
rather than the blue;
Sad or sunny musing
Is largely in the choosing,
And just being happy
is brave work and true.

Just being happy
helps other souls along;
Their burdens may be heavy
and they not strong;
And your own sky will lighten,
If other skies you brighten
By just being happy
with a heart full of song.

RIPLEY D. SAUNDERS

The Comfort Room

∽ Mayo Mathers ∽

"Is your Comfort Room available next weekend?" The voice of my friend on the telephone sounded weary and faint. "I could sure use a respite."

I smiled, assuring her it was. Hanging up the phone, I walked down the hall to the room she'd inquired about. The Comfort Room developed quite by accident, but there is no doubt in my mind that the people who stay here are no accident at all. God brings them to us when they're most in need of comfort.

I looked around the room, running my hand lightly across the soothing pattern of the wallpaper. Walking over to the antique bed, I stretched out across the quilt with its blue and white wedding ring pattern and luxuriated in the familiar sense of comfort that settled over me like a feathery eiderdown.

My earliest memory of the bed goes back to when I was three years old. My parents had just brought my new baby sister to Grandma's house where I'd been staying. As Mom laid her on the bed, I stood on my tiptoes, eagerly peeking over the high mattress to catch a glimpse of her.

For as long as I can remember, the bed and its accompanying dresser and dressing table occupied what had once been the parlor of my grandparents' large Missouri farmhouse. During those long-ago summers, when all the grandchildren visited, "taking turns" was the order of the day. We took turns on the porch swing, took turns on the bicycle, and even took turns at the chores. But there was no taking turns when it came to sleeping in Grandma's bed. Even on hot, smothery, summer nights she let us all pile in around her at once. Our sweaty little bodies stuck happily together as we listened to Grandma's beloved stories of the "olden days" until one by one, we fell asleep.

Those well-spun tales gave me a strong sense of family identity, pride, and comfort. And I needed plenty of comfort when clouds started building in the summery blue skies that stretched over the corn fields surrounding the farm. How I dreaded the wild, crashing, earsplitting midwestern thunderstorms that resulted from those massive clouds!

Standing at the window, I'd watch the lightning flashes intensify across the sky and count the seconds until I heard the low growl of thunder. Grandma told me that was how to tell how many miles away the storm was.

I hated nighttime storms the most—when I'd have to go upstairs to my bedroom, up even closer to the storm. Sleep was impossible. As the jagged slashes grew more brilliant, the time between the stab of lightning and the crash of thunder grew less and less.

Then suddenly, *flash! ka-a-a-boom!* The light and sound came as one! The storm was here! Right on top of me! At that point, I'd leap from the bed, and with my sister close behind, we'd slam into our brother in the hallway. The three of us tore down the stairs as one.

Hearing our pounding feet, Grandma would already be scooted over in bed with the covers thrown back for us. We plowed beneath them, scrunching up as close to her as we could. While the thunder shook and rattled the house, she'd jump dramatically and exclaim, "Whew! That one made my whiskers grow!"

And from under the pillows where we'd buried our heads, we couldn't help but giggle. In Grandma's bed we were always comforted.

There I found comfort not only from thunderstorms but from lifestorms as well. Hurt feelings, broken hearts, insecurities—all were mended there. When I was lucky enough to have Grandma to myself in her bed—which wasn't often—I'd tell her all my deepest secrets, knowing she took them very seriously.

When my father, her son, died of cancer, I was eight years old. On that last night of his life, instead of spending those moments with him in the hospital, Grandma gathered me into her bed. Curling her body around mine, she infused me with comfort I didn't yet know I needed.

In college, when a broken engagement had crushed my heart and hopes, she comforted me by saying, "The pathway to love never runs smooth, honey, but you'll find your way when it's right." Four years later, her prediction came true.

Shortly after my wedding, Grandma died, bringing an end to the unlimited source of love and comfort that I knew could never be replaced, the kind that only comes from a grandmother. When my aunt called to tell me the beloved bedroom set was mine, I immediately drove to Missouri to pick it up. Although the beautiful pieces had to be placed in storage, I hoped that someday I'd have room for them in our home.

The years melted away with startling speed. Caught up in the happy frenzy of raising our two sons, I rarely thought of the bedroom set stuck away in the attic. There was too much present to think of the past. Before I knew it, our firstborn was packing his belongings to move on to a new phase of life.

The day Tyler left, I went into his empty room and sat down in the middle of the floor while memory after memory scurried up to tap me on the shoulder. His leave-taking had been more wrenching than I had anticipated. Inside the echoes of the room I tried to come to grips with the door that had just closed on my life.

Quite abruptly, a thought came to mind. I raised my head and looked around my son's room with new eyes. I finally had room for Grandma's bedroom set!

For the next two weeks I worked on the room, lovingly choosing paint, wallpaper, and pictures. Frequent tears splashed into the paint tray as I pondered all the different seasons one passes through in a lifetime. When the painting and papering were done, my husband lugged the bedroom set down from the attic and helped me arrange it in the room. I stopped to consider the completed result and was drawn to the bed where I let my fingers trace around the grooves in the curved footboard of the wonderful old treasure. As I sat quietly, a familiar feeling begged to embrace me—the same feeling I'd had as a child with Grandma beside me in the bed. It was as if she were in the room with me right then comforting me in this new stage of life I was entering.

Right then I christened it the "Comfort Room." From where I sat I prayed, "Lord, I hope everyone who stays in this room feels the comfort I'm feeling now. Bring people to us who need the comfort."

Our first guest in the Comfort Room was a friend who'd just lost her brother and two close friends to death. Next was a couple who were at a transition point in their life, not sure which direction to go. Then a young cousin arrived in need of a temporary home and an out-of-town uncle whose wife was flown to our medical center following a severe heart attack. From the day it was completed, God has seen to it that the Comfort Room is well used.

There is one guest, however, whose arrival I most anticipate. I'm waiting for the day when my son will return and bring with him a grandchild. Then I will be the grandma snuggling up with my grandchild in that old bed. I'll be the one spinning stories of the "olden days." And I'll offer to them what my grandma gave to me—unending comfort, unlimited love.

Grandma's Glasses

PHIL CALLAWAY

from *Who Put the Skunk in the Trunk?*

Two eight-year-olds were talking after school one day. The one asked the other, "Wouldn't you hate to wear glasses all the time?"

The other responded, "Nope. Not if I had the kind Grandma wears. She sees how to fix lots of stuff, and she sees lots of cool things to do on rainy days, and she sees when folks are tired and sad, and what will make them feel better, and she always sees what you meant to do even if you haven't gotten things right just yet. I asked her one day how she could see that way, and she said it was the way she had learned to look at things when she got older. So it must be her glasses."

Heart of the Matter

Teaching creative writing to an elementary school class, I closed with a question: "How do you know your grandmother loves you?" A little boy waved his hand with enthusiasm. When I called on him, he said, "I know my grandma loves me 'cause when I look in her eyes, I can see all the way to her heart."

AUTHOR UNKNOWN

Angel In Uniform

Jeannie Ecke Sowell

This is a family story my father told me about his mother, my grandmother.

In 1949 my father had just returned home from the war. On every American highway you could see the soldiers in uniform hitchhiking home to their families, as was the custom at that time in America.

Sadly, the thrill of his reunion with his family was soon overshadowed. My grandmother became very ill and had to be hospitalized. It was her kidneys, and the doctors told my father that she needed a blood transfusion immediately or she would not live through the night. The problem was that Grandmother's blood type was AB-, a very rare type even today, but even harder to get then because there were no blood banks or air flights to ship blood. All the family members were typed, but not one member was a match. So the doctors gave the family no hope; my grandmother was dying.

My father left the hospital in tears to gather up all the family members, so that everyone would get a chance to tell Grandmother good-bye. As my father was driving down the highway, he passed a soldier in uniform hitchhiking home to his family. Deep in grief, my father had no inclination at that moment to do a good deed. Yet it was almost as if something outside himself pulled him to a stop, and he waited as the stranger climbed into the car.

My father was too upset to even ask the soldier his name, but the soldier noticed my father's tears right away and inquired about them. Through his tears, my father told this stranger that his mother was lying in a hospital dying because the doctors had been unable to locate her blood type, AB-, and if they did not locate her blood type before nightfall, she would surely die.

It got very quiet in the car. Then this

unidentified soldier extended his hand out to my father, palm up. Resting in the palm of his hand were the dog tags from around his neck. The blood type on the tags was AB-. The soldier told my father to turn the car around and get him to the hospital.

My grandmother lived until 1996, forty-seven years later, and to this day no one in the family knows this soldier's name. But my father has often wondered, was he a soldier or an angel in uniform?

Love seeketh not itself to please, nor for itself hath any care, but for another gives its ease, and builds a Heaven in Hell's despair.

WILLIAM BLAKE

Stitches in Time

PHILIP GULLEY
from *Home Town Tales*

Electricity was discovered by the ancient Greeks, though it didn't find its way to my in-laws' farm until the summer of 1948. That's when the truck from the Orange County Rural Electric Cooperative made its way down Grimes Lake Road, planting poles and stringing wire.

My mother-in-law, Ruby, sat on her front porch snapping beans while the linemen set the poles. That night she asked her husband, Howard, what he thought of her getting an electric sewing machine. Her treadle sewing machine was broken, the victim of two high-spirited boys who had pumped the treadle to an early death.

They drove to Bedford the next day to the Singer Sewing Center and bought a brand-new electric Singer with a buttonholer, a cabinet, and a chair. It cost two hundred and forty dollars, money they'd earned from selling a truckload of hogs to the meatpacking plant in New Solsberry.

Ruby set in to sewing for her boys. They added three children to their flock. More sewing. After supper, when the table was cleared and dishes washed, Ruby would bend over the machine, churning out clothes for her children and her neighbors. Thousands of dresses and shirts and pants. Clothes for dolls. Clothes for the minister's wife in town. Prom dresses. Wedding dresses. The Singer raised its needle millions of times. Her family would fall asleep under Ruby-made quilts, lulled to sleep by the Singer hum.

The kids grew up and moved away. Grandchildren came, eight in all. The Singer stitched maternity clothes, baby dresses, baptismal gowns, and quilts for the cribs. In 1987, Ruby called us on the phone, discouraged. After thirty-nine years, her

Singer was limping. She took it to Mr. Gardner in the next town over. He fixed sewing machines but couldn't revive hers. He sent it away to Chicago. A month later it came back, a paper tag hanging from its cord. *Obsolete. Parts not available,* the tag read.

I went to a sewing machine store the next day to buy a new one. Her old one was metal. The new machines are plastic and have computers and cost the same as Ruby's first car. They give classes on how to use them. In the display window was a 1948 metal Singer blackhead.

"Does that one work?" I asked the man.

"I don't know," he said. "Let's plug it in." He plugged it in. It hummed to life.

"It's not for sale," he told me. "It's a display. There aren't a lot of these old Singer blackheads around anymore."

I told him about Ruby—how she lives by herself and sews to keep busy, how she only charges six dollars to make a dress because the people she sews for don't have a lot of money, how a lot of times she doesn't charge a dime, how sewing is her ministry.

He sold the machine to me for twenty-five dollars.

The next weekend we hauled it down to Ruby's. She was sitting on the front porch, watching for our car to round the corner on the gravel lane. She came outside and stood by the car as we opened the trunk. As she peered down at the '48 blackhead, a smile creased her face.

"It's just like my old one," she whispered.

We wrestled it inside and installed it in her old cabinet. Perfect fit. Plugged it in. When Ruby heard the hum, she clapped her hands.

It's still going strong. Ruby still charges six dollars a dress—unless it's a bride's dress; then she sews it by hand. That'll cost you fifteen dollars, but only if you can afford it.

Ruby travels north to visit her granddaughter Rachael. Rachael shows Ruby her Barbie doll, then asks Ruby if she could maybe please sew some clothes for Barbie. The first night Ruby is home, she bends over her '48 blackhead, stitching matching dresses for Rachael and her Barbie. Way past midnight she sews. The next morning she drives to town and mails a package northward. Three days later the phone rings. It's Rachael calling to say "Thank you" and "I love you" and "When can I see you again?"

On two other occasions, my wife and I found 1948 Singer blackheads in antique stores. We bought them and gave them to Ruby. She's got a lot of sewing ahead, and we don't want her to run out of sewing machines before she runs out of things to sew.

I don't always applaud every new thing that comes down the road, though I'm grateful that in 1948 electricity made its way down Grimes Lake Road. I'm grateful, too, for a woman who sews way into the night, who dispenses love one stitch at a time.

ᕦᘎᕤ

In the end, it's not the years
in your life that count. It's the
life in your years.

Abraham Lincoln

Grandma's Gift

∽ Wayne Rice ∽

As a ninth grader, Dave was the smallest kid in his high school. But at five feet tall and ninety pounds, he was the perfect candidate for the lightest weight class on the school's wrestling team. Dave started out as the JV lightweight, but moved up to the varsity position when the boy at the spot moved away.

Unfortunately, Dave's first year was not one for the record books. Of the six varsity matches he wrestled, he was pinned six times.

Dave had a dream of someday being a good enough wrestler to receive his athlete's letter. An athlete's letter is a cloth emblem with the school's initials on it, which is awarded to those athletes who demonstrate exceptional performance in their sports. Those who were fortunate enough to receive a letter proudly wore it on their school letterman jackets.

Whenever Dave shared his dream of lettering in wrestling, most of his teammates and friends just laughed. Those who did offer encouragement to Dave usually said something like, "Well, it's not whether you win or lose…" or "It's not really important whether you letter or not…." Even so, Dave was determined to work hard and keep improving as a wrestler.

Every day after school, Dave was in the weight room trying to build up his strength, or running the stadium bleachers trying to increase his endurance, or in the wrestling room trying to improve his technique.

The one person who continually believed in Dave was his

grandmother. Every time she saw him she reminded him of what could be done through prayer and hard work. She told him to keep focused on his goal. Over and over again, she quoted Bible verses to him, like "I can do all things through Christ who gives me strength!"(Philippians 4:13).

The day before the next season began, Dave's grandmother passed away. He was heartbroken. If he ever did reach his goal of someday getting a high school letter, his grandmother would never know.

That season Dave's opponents faced a new person. What they expected was an easy victory. What they got instead was a ferocious battle. Dave won nine of his first ten matches that year.

Midway through the season, Dave's coach called him into his office to inform him that he would be receiving his high school letter. Dave was ecstatic. The only thing that could have made him feel better was to be able to share it with his grandmother. If only she knew!

Just then the coach smiled as he presented Dave with an envelope. The envelope had Dave's name written on it in his grandmother's handwriting.

He opened it and read:

Dear Dave,

I knew you could do it! I set aside $100 to buy you a school jacket to put your letter on. I hope you'll wear it proudly, and remember, "You can do all things through Christ who gives you strength!"

Congratulations,

Grandma

After Dave finished reading the letter, his coach reached behind him and pulled out a brandnew jacket with the school letter attached and Dave's name embroidered on the front. Dave realized then that his grandmother did know after all.

❧

A place in thy memory, Dearest!
Is all that I claim!
To pause and look back when thou hearest
The Sound of my name.

GERALD GRIFFIN

Breaking Up Grandma

Marjorie Maki

The terrible twos stretched into the threes for me. An only child whose mother was ill and hospitalized a good share of the time, I was watched by various relatives. But I missed my mama dreadfully, and acted accordingly. Apparently the only one who could cope with me was my grandmother in Wisconsin.

Grandma was a big strong Norwegian lady who raised eight children and milked nine cows the day after each child was born.

Once when she came to take care of me in our small home on the east side of St. Paul, I proceeded to make her life miserable. When she tried to take me for a walk, I'd scoot ahead of her at surprising speed, leaving her to chase me on her fifty-eight-year-old legs. When she devised an effective harness, I plunked down on the grass in our front yard and yelled. When she called me to eat lunch, I'd squeeze under my parents' iron bed, pulling down the chenille bedspread, or hide behind the brown overstuffed chair in the corner.

It all came to an end the day Grandma decided to soothe me once more in our old black wooden rocking chair. She had patience and lots of love, so she held me in her arms and sang songs from her childhood by the sea.

I was not impressed. I couldn't get away, and I still didn't like it. I pulled tendrils of gray hair out of her neat bun, poked an inquisitive finger up her nose and jabbed her cheeks. Her blue eyes remained amazingly calm. Finally, I slipped my fingers into her mouth. Instantly the singing stopped, and she wiggled her jaw in a funny way.

My hand came out holding her false teeth!

Shocked, I stared at the ugly things, dropped them and started screaming.

I cried for an hour. In between sobs I would hug her and ask if she hurt. I kept hiccuping, "I'm sorry, I'm sorry." She rocked me contentedly.

My terrible threes ended that day.

You know, people have to be treated nice.

They break into little pieces if you don't.

Love is patient, love is kind.

1 CORINTHIANS 13:4, NIV

The greatest use of life is to spend it for
something that will outlast it.

WILLIAM JAMES

Written from the Heart

～ BOB WELCH ～

Near as anyone can tell, Sally's grandmother never touched a computer keyboard. She didn't particularly like talking on the phone. Instead, she communicated with her extended family through something far superior to anything high technology could offer, something better than even e-mail.

She reached out and touched us all with g-mail—Gram Mail.

Gram Youngberg, who died in the fall of 1997 at the age of ninety-five, wrote letters. Thousands of letters spanning decades and decades, many of which my wife has saved. Part of Gram's legacy was how she lived her life, but part of it, too, was the words she left with us all—words that became an extension of the woman who penned them.

Words that helped sustain and link the interdependent parts of her legacy tree.

They tell us of a simple, salt-of-the-earth woman who noticed the daily comings and goings of people with detailed enthusiasm. Like Emily, the young girl in Our Town who wonders if anyone but the "saints and poets" really notice the nuances of life around them, Gram, too, noticed the "clocks ticking, and Mama's sunflowers and new-ironed dresses and hot baths…." Mainly, she noticed her extended family and friends.

"Bud Payne," she wrote in one letter, "is still housebound with his severed knee ligament… Max Coffey plans on going to Haiti as a mechanic on the medical team the last of November… My, but Brad and Paul have grown!…"

The letters tell of someone for whom people were the utmost priority. She always wrote more about others than herself. She gloried in her family's victories, commiserated in our defeats. She welcomed in-laws into the family as if we

69

were long-lost friends who, despite no blood links, belonged. She was always more amazed at the accomplishments of others than of her own, though she had many.

"Sally: We are so proud of you and Ann for doing your bit for others in Haiti…."

"Today, I've been painting the little wooden fire trucks, eleven of them, for needy children. Then sand them and paint again. Takes almost twenty minutes to do one."

The letters tell of someone who had a special heart for children.

"I'm enjoying my Sunday School class. I have eight, five- and six-year-olds and they are nice little kids."

"Your boys' drawings are something. Ryan's cows are an active, happy bunch, and show such action."

The letters tell of someone who reveled in the bounty of God's earth, in weather and soil and seasons and sunsets. "I'm busy with Indian summer crops," she wrote. "I love this time of year. Freezing corn, drying prunes, and finishing up on canning.

The apple crop—pears also—were nothing and the few on the trees were wormy and scaly. But there are peaches. And how we enjoyed them!"

In another letter: "Thermometer showed twenty degrees and white frost. Snow in the hills but not here—yet." And still another: "Have you been seeing the glorious sunsets: one last night—and then sunsets during the week. They are gorgeous to behold—to appreciate the handiwork of the Lord."

Her letters were full of recipes and news of chickens and cows and gophers and sewing and church potlucks and, of course, Pop. She always took time to ask about how your family was doing. She was fond of exclamation points and, for rare occasions (like when noting a granddaughter's husband was home from the service), used happy faces.

She seldom complained. Oh, a few letters included touching lines in the years after Pop died; she was lonely. But for the most part, she had an uncanny ability to see silver linings in the darkest of clouds, to accept that pain and loss were part of life, much as drought and hail were part of farming.

"Pop is tired," she once wrote, "but we can't complain."

From another letter, extolling the accomplishments of other family members: "Aren't we lucky."

Were Gram alive today, I know how she would respond to such glowing accounts of her life. She would react the same way she reacted after I told her what an inspiration she was and that I felt fortunate to be part of her family, even as an adjunct. "Thanks for the complimentary letter, Bob, but to be honest, I'm very undeserving of such noble motives. For I'm doing what comes naturally. In my growing-up years, I learned to make do, to make use of what is on hand, so I do it."

Decades of letters. Letters whose stamps, in just the last twenty-five years, went from eight cents to thirty-two cents. Letters that, for a while, after Gram broke her arm, were written left-handed. Letters first signed "Gram and Pop" then just "Gram," then finally stopped coming altogether—but only when she physically could no longer write.

Letters reminding us that, over the years, Gram really had two gardens: one with carrots and peas and tomatoes and corn. And one with a son and two daughters and grandchildren and great-grandchildren and nieces and nephews.

In addressing the church at Corinth, Paul writes, "You yourselves are our letter, written on our hearts, known and read by everybody." In a sense, Gram's life was one long love letter to her family and friends and God. A ninety-five-year-long letter.

Nothing would make her prouder than to know that we had tucked that letter in our wallets and purses—better yet, hidden it in our hearts—and lived the same kind of other-oriented life she had lived. She would want us to look for the best in one another. To "make do" with what circumstances we've been given. And, of course, to stop and look at the sunrises and sunsets, for, as she wrote, "They are gorgeous to behold…the handiwork of the Lord."

Always a Blessing

The reason God made grandmas is they are sweet,
They comfort you when you're down,
And most of all, because they love you.

BREANAH SHANTEL GRAY, *age eight*

As we skipped down a road bordered by summer wild flowers, my granddaughter asked, "Grandma, are you young or are you old?" With a twinkle in my eyes, I answered with words someone else said: "Precious one, Grandma has been young for a very, very, very long time!"

ALICE GRAY

I didn't know if my granddaughter had learned her colors yet, so I decided to test her. I would point out something and ask what color it was. She would tell me, and always she was correct. But it was fun for me, so I continued. At last she headed for the door, saying sagely, "Grandma, I think you should try to figure out some of these yourself!"

SAMUEL SMILES

Grandmothers are just antique little girls.

AUTHOR UNKNOWN

WALKING WITH GRANDMA

I like to walk with Grandma,

Her steps are short like mine.

She doesn't say, "Now hurry up,"

She always takes her time.

I like to walk with Grandma,

Her eyes see things like mine do.

Wee pebble bright, a funny cloud,

Half hidden drops of dew.

Most people have to hurry,

They do not stop and see...

I'm glad that God made Grandma,

Unrushed and young like me.

· AUTHOR UNKNOWN

The task ahead of us is never as great as the power behind us.

RALPH WALDO EMERSON

Acknowledgments

A diligent search has been made to trace original ownership, and when necessary, permission to reprint has been obtained. If I have overlooked giving proper credit to anyone, please accept my apologies. Should any attribution be found to be incorrect, the publisher welcomes written documentation supporting correction for subsequent printings. For material not in the public domain, grateful acknowledgment is given to the publishers and individuals who have granted permission for use of their material.

Acknowledgments are listed by story title in the order they appear in the book. For permission to reprint any of the stories please request permission from the original source listed below.

"A Day Hemmed in Love" by Nancy Jo Sullivan. Taken from *Moments of Grace* by Nancy Jo Sullivan, © 2000. Used by permission of Multnomah Publishers, Inc.

"Grandmas Make a Difference" by Betty Southard, © 1996. Used by permission of the author.

"Love is a Grandparent" by Erma Bombeck from *Forever, Erma* © 1996 by the Estate of Erma Bombeck. Reprinted with permission of Andrews McMeel Publishing. All rights reserved.

"Lilacs to Remember" by Faith Andrews Bedford. This story was first published in *Country Living*, where her column, "Kids in the Country" appears regularly. Used by permission of the author.

"Bouquet of Love" by John R. Ramsey. © 1997. Used by permission of the author.

"Stories on a Headboard" by Elaine Pondant. Originally appeared in the August 1993 *HomeLife*. Reprinted with permission from the March 1994 *Reader's Digest* and from the August 1993 *HomeLife*, © 1993 The Sunday School Board of the Southern Baptist Convention. All rights reserved. Used by permission.

"A Gift to Remember" by Corrie Frantz Cowart. © 1997. Used by permission of the author. Corrie Franz Cowart is from Corbett, Oregon. She is a freelance writer, dancer, and choreographer currently living in Eugene, OR.

"Grandma's Laughter" by Casandra Lindell, freelance writer and editor, Lake Oswego, OR. © 1998. Used by permission of the author.

"The Attic Dance" by Robin Jones Gunn, © 2000. Used by permission of the author. Robin Jones Gunn is the bestselling author of the the Glenbrooke series by Multnomah Publishers, Inc., and the Christy Miller series by Bethany House Publishers.

"When Grandma Grows Up" by Marilyn McAuley, © 1995. Used by permission of the author. Marilyn is a freelance writer and copyeditor living in Vancouver, WA.

"Mother Earned Her Wrinkles" by Erma Bombeck from *Forever, Erma* © 1996 by the Estate of Erma Bombeck. Reprinted